Living with Bipolar Disorder:
Understanding, Diagnosing and Managing Bipolar Disorder

By Courtney Collins

Living with Bipolar Disorder

© 2024 by Courtney Collins

All rights reserved. No part of this publication may be reproduced, distributed, or transmitted in any form or by any means, including photocopying, recording, or other electronic or mechanical methods, without the prior written permission of the publisher, except in the case of brief quotations embodied in critical reviews and certain other non-commercial uses allowed by copyright law.

Table of Contents

Introduction to Bipolar Disorder 5

Understanding the Types of Bipolar Disorder 7

Recognizing the Symptoms 9

Diagnosis: The Journey to Understanding 11

The Science Behind Bipolar Disorder 13

Medication Management 15

Therapy Options: Finding the Right Fit 17

Lifestyle Changes and Self-Care 19

Managing Manic Episodes 21

Coping with Depressive Episodes 22

The Role of Support Systems 23

Bipolar Disorder in Relationships 24

Navigating Work and Bipolar Disorder 25

Long-Term Management and Prognosis 27

Personal Stories and Inspiration 28

Parenting with Bipolar Disorder 30

Bipolar Disorder and Creativity 32

Personal Stories and Inspiration 34

Living with Bipolar Disorder

Chapter 1:

Introduction to Bipolar Disorder

What is Bipolar Disorder?

Bipolar disorder, formerly known as manic-depressive illness, is a chronic mental health condition characterized by extreme mood swings. These mood swings range from periods of intense mania or hypomania to episodes of deep depression. The fluctuation between these emotional highs and lows can be distressing and can disrupt an individual's daily life, relationships, and work.

Historical Perspective

Bipolar disorder has been recognized for centuries, although it was not always understood in the way it is today. Ancient texts from Greece and Rome described symptoms that align with what we now know as bipolar disorder. The term "manic-depressive illness" was coined in the early 20th century by German psychiatrist Emil Kraepelin. It was not until the late 20th century that the term "bipolar disorder" became more widely used, reflecting a broader understanding of the condition.

Prevalence and Impact

Bipolar disorder affects approximately 1-3% of the global population. It can manifest at any age, though it typically appears in late adolescence or early adulthood. The disorder has significant personal, social, and economic impacts. Untreated, it can lead to substance abuse, financial problems, damaged relationships, and increased risk of suicide. However, with effective treatment, many individuals with bipolar disorder can lead productive and fulfilling lives.

Case Study: Maria's Journey

Maria, a 28-year-old marketing executive, began experiencing mood swings in her early twenties. She would have weeks of high energy, where she felt unstoppable and took on numerous projects, followed by periods of deep sadness and hopelessness. After several years of struggling, Maria sought help and was diagnosed with Bipolar II Disorder. With a combination of medication, therapy, and lifestyle changes, Maria has learned to manage her symptoms and maintain her career.

Chapter 2:

Understanding the Types of Bipolar Disorder

Bipolar I Disorder

Bipolar I Disorder is characterized by manic episodes that last at least seven days or by manic symptoms that are so severe that immediate hospital care is needed. Depressive episodes often occur as well, typically lasting at least two weeks. Some people may also experience mixed episodes, which involve both manic and depressive symptoms simultaneously.

Bipolar II Disorder

Bipolar II Disorder involves a pattern of depressive episodes and hypomanic episodes, which are less severe than the full-blown manic episodes of Bipolar I. Hypomania may not cause the significant impairment that mania does, but it still represents a marked change in mood and behaviour that can be distressing.

Cyclothymic Disorder

Cyclothymic disorder, or cyclothymia, is a milder form of bipolar disorder. Individuals with cyclothymia experience chronic fluctuating moods involving periods of hypomanic symptoms and periods of depressive symptoms for at least two years (one year in children and adolescents). These symptoms are not severe enough to meet the criteria for a hypomanic or depressive episode.

Other Specified and Unspecified Bipolar and Related Disorders

These categories are used when symptoms do not match the criteria for the aforementioned types but still involve significant mood disturbances. They include disorders with short-duration hypomanic episodes and major depressive episodes, as well as those with hypomanic episodes without prior depressive episodes.

Case Study: John's Experience

John, a 35-year-old teacher, was diagnosed with Bipolar I Disorder after a particularly severe manic episode led to hospitalization. His manic phase included impulsive decisions, reckless spending, and unrealistic plans. Following this, he experienced a deep depressive episode that made it difficult to get out of bed or engage in daily activities. With the help of his psychiatrist, John has found a medication regimen that stabilizes his mood, and he attends regular therapy sessions to manage his condition.

Chapter 3:

Recognizing the Symptoms

Manic and Hypomanic Episodes

During a manic episode, individuals may feel euphoric, full of energy, or unusually irritable. Symptoms include:

- Inflated self-esteem or grandiosity

- Decreased need for sleep

- More talkative than usual or pressure to keep talking

- Flight of ideas or subjective experience that thoughts are racing

- Distractibility

- Increase in goal-directed activity or psychomotor agitation

- Excessive involvement in activities that have a high potential for painful consequences (e.g., unrestrained spending sprees, sexual indiscretions)

Hypomania is similar to mania but less severe and without psychotic features. The symptoms last for at least four days and do not cause significant impairment in social or occupational functioning.

Depressive Episodes

Depressive episodes are characterized by:

- Depressed mood most of the day, nearly every day

- Markedly diminished interest or pleasure in all, or almost all, activities most of the day

- Significant weight loss when not dieting, weight gain, or decrease or increase in appetite

- Insomnia or hypersomnia

- Psychomotor agitation or retardation

- Fatigue or loss of energy

- Feelings of worthlessness or excessive or inappropriate guilt

- Diminished ability to think or concentrate, or indecisiveness

- Recurrent thoughts of death, recurrent suicidal ideation without a specific plan, or a suicide attempt or a specific plan for committing suicide

Mixed Features

Mixed features occur when symptoms of both mania and depression are present nearly every day for at least one week. This can be particularly challenging to manage because it involves the high energy of mania coupled with the negative mood of depression.

Case Study: Sarah's Struggle

Sarah, a 22-year-old college student, experienced severe mood swings that impacted her academic performance and social life. During manic episodes, she would stay up all night working on projects, feel overly confident, and make impulsive decisions. Her depressive episodes made it hard to get out of bed, causing her to miss classes and withdraw from friends. After being diagnosed with Bipolar II Disorder, Sarah started a treatment plan that included medication and therapy, helping her achieve more stability.

Chapter 4:

Diagnosis: The Journey to Understanding

Initial Consultation

The diagnostic process typically begins with a visit to a healthcare provider, such as a primary care physician or a psychiatrist. The initial consultation involves discussing the individual's symptoms, medical history, and any relevant family history of mental health issues. This step is crucial to rule out other medical conditions that might mimic bipolar disorder, such as thyroid disorders or neurological conditions.

Diagnostic Criteria

The Diagnostic and Statistical Manual of Mental Disorders (DSM-5) outlines specific criteria for diagnosing bipolar disorder. For Bipolar I Disorder, the criteria include at least one manic episode, which may be preceded or followed by hypomanic or major depressive episodes. For Bipolar II Disorder, the criteria include at least one hypomanic episode and one major depressive episode, with no history of a manic episode.

Assessment Tools

Various assessment tools and questionnaires can aid in the diagnostic process. The Mood Disorder Questionnaire (MDQ) is a common screening tool that helps identify symptoms of bipolar disorder. Additionally, the Young Mania Rating Scale (YMRS) and the Hamilton Depression Rating Scale (HDRS) are used to assess the severity of manic and depressive symptoms, respectively.

Importance of Accurate Diagnosis

Accurate diagnosis is crucial for effective treatment planning and management. Misdiagnosis can lead to inappropriate treatment, such as prescribing antidepressants without mood stabilizers, which can trigger manic episodes in individuals with bipolar disorder. An accurate diagnosis allows for a tailored treatment approach that addresses the specific needs of the individual.

Case Study: David's Path to Diagnosis

David, a 40-year-old accountant, had experienced mood swings for years but was initially misdiagnosed with major depressive disorder. He was prescribed antidepressants, which exacerbated his manic symptoms. After a particularly severe manic episode, David sought a second opinion and was diagnosed with Bipolar I Disorder. His new treatment plan included mood stabilizers and antipsychotic medications, which helped him achieve better mood stability.

Chapter 5:

The Science Behind Bipolar Disorder

Genetic Factors

Research indicates that bipolar disorder has a significant genetic component. Studies of families, twins, and adoption cases have shown that individuals with a first-degree relative (parent or sibling) with bipolar disorder have a higher risk of developing the condition. However, genetics alone do not account for the development of bipolar disorder; environmental factors also play a crucial role.

Neurobiological Factors

Neuroimaging studies have revealed structural and functional differences in the brains of individuals with bipolar disorder. Areas such as the prefrontal cortex, which is involved in executive functions and emotional regulation, show altered activity. Additionally, there is evidence of dysregulation in neurotransmitter systems, including dopamine, serotonin, and norepinephrine, which are crucial for mood regulation.

Environmental Triggers

While genetics and neurobiology set the stage, environmental triggers often play a pivotal role in the onset of bipolar disorder. Stressful life events, trauma, and substance abuse are known triggers. For instance, a significant life change, such as the death of a loved one or a major career setback, can precipitate a mood episode in someone predisposed to bipolar disorder.

Case Study: Emily's Triggers

Emily, a 30-year-old writer, had a family history of bipolar disorder. Her symptoms began after she experienced the trauma of a severe car accident. The stress and physical recovery process triggered her first manic episode. Understanding the interplay of genetic predisposition and environmental triggers helped Emily and her healthcare providers develop a comprehensive treatment plan.

Chapter 6:

Medication Management

Mood Stabilizers

Mood stabilizers are the cornerstone of pharmacological treatment for bipolar disorder. Lithium is one of the oldest and most effective mood stabilizers, particularly for preventing manic episodes. Anticonvulsants, such as valproate, lamotrigine, and carbamazepine, are also commonly used and can help stabilize mood swings.

Antipsychotics

Atypical antipsychotics, such as quetiapine, olanzapine, and aripiprazole, are often used to manage acute manic or mixed episodes. They can also be effective in treating bipolar depression. These medications work by altering the activity of certain neurotransmitters in the brain.

Antidepressants

Antidepressants may be used cautiously in bipolar disorder, typically in combination with a mood stabilizer to prevent triggering manic episodes. Selective serotonin reuptake inhibitors (SSRIs) and serotonin-norepinephrine reuptake inhibitors (SNRIs) are commonly prescribed.

Medication Adherence

Adherence to medication is critical for managing symptoms and preventing relapse. Non-adherence is a common issue, often due to side effects, lack of insight into the illness, or a desire to experience the highs of mania. Education and a strong therapeutic alliance between the patient and healthcare provider can improve adherence.

Case Study: Mark's Treatment Plan

Mark, a 45-year-old engineer, struggled with medication adherence due to the side effects of his mood stabilizers. He worked with his psychiatrist to find a combination of medications that managed his symptoms with minimal side effects. Regular follow-ups and a strong support system helped Mark stay on track with his treatment plan, leading to improved stability and quality of life.

Chapter 7:

Therapy Options: Finding the Right Fit

Cognitive Behavioural Therapy (CBT)

CBT is a widely used therapy for bipolar disorder. It helps individuals identify and change negative thought patterns and behaviours. CBT can be particularly effective in managing depressive episodes by addressing distorted thinking and fostering problem-solving skills.

Interpersonal and Social Rhythm Therapy (IPSRT)

IPSRT focuses on stabilizing daily routines and improving interpersonal relationships. The therapy aims to regulate daily activities, such as sleeping, eating, and socializing, which can help stabilize mood swings. It also addresses interpersonal issues that may contribute to stress and mood disturbances.

Family-Focused Therapy

Family-focused therapy involves family members in treatment to improve communication, problem-solving, and support. This approach can be particularly beneficial in reducing relapse rates and improving overall family functioning. Educating family members about bipolar disorder helps them understand the condition and how to provide effective support.

Other Therapies

Dialectical behaviour therapy (DBT) and psychoeducation are also beneficial for individuals with bipolar disorder. DBT focuses on teaching coping skills to manage intense emotions and reduce self-destructive behaviours. Psychoeducation involves educating individuals and their families about bipolar disorder, treatment options, and strategies for managing the condition.

Case Study: Linda's Therapeutic Journey

Linda, a 38-year-old artist, was initially resistant to therapy, believing that medication alone would suffice. After experiencing several relapses, she began attending CBT sessions. Through therapy, Linda learned to recognize early warning signs of mood episodes and developed strategies to manage stress. Incorporating family-focused therapy helped improve her relationships and provided her with a robust support network.

Chapter 8:

Lifestyle Changes and Self-Care

Sleep Hygiene

Maintaining a regular sleep schedule is crucial for mood stability. Going to bed and waking up at the same time each day helps regulate the body's internal clock. Avoiding caffeine and electronic devices before bedtime can also improve sleep quality.

Diet and Exercise

A balanced diet and regular exercise can positively impact mood and overall well-being. Omega-3 fatty acids, found in fish and flaxseed, have been shown to have mood-stabilizing effects. Regular physical activity, such as walking, yoga, or swimming, releases endorphins that improve mood and reduce stress.

Stress Management

Techniques such as mindfulness, meditation, and relaxation exercises can help manage stress. Mindfulness involves staying present in the moment and can reduce the impact of stressors. Meditation practices, such as deep breathing and guided imagery, promote relaxation and emotional balance.

Avoiding Substance Abuse

Substance abuse can worsen bipolar symptoms and interfere with treatment. Alcohol and recreational drugs can trigger mood episodes and complicate the management of the disorder. Seeking support for substance abuse issues is vital for maintaining stability.

Case Study: Jessica's Lifestyle Transformation

Jessica, a 29-year-old nurse, experienced frequent mood swings despite taking medication. Her psychiatrist recommended lifestyle changes to complement her treatment. Jessica began practicing good sleep hygiene, incorporating regular exercise into her routine, and attending mindfulness classes. These changes significantly improved her mood stability and overall quality of life.

Chapter 9:

Managing Manic Episodes

Early Warning Signs

Recognizing early warning signs of mania, such as increased energy, reduced need for sleep, and heightened irritability, can help prevent full-blown episodes. Keeping a mood diary can help identify these signs early on.

Strategies for Control

Strategies for managing mania include sticking to a routine, avoiding overstimulation, and having a plan in place for when symptoms escalate. Techniques such as deep breathing, grounding exercises, and taking breaks can help manage stress and overstimulation.

Seeking Help

Promptly seeking help from a healthcare provider can prevent a manic episode from worsening. Adjustments to medication, additional therapy sessions, or temporary hospitalization may be necessary.

Case Study: Paul's Manic Episode

Paul, a 34-year-old entrepreneur, noticed early signs of mania, such as racing thoughts and impulsive spending. Recognizing these signs from previous episodes, he immediately contacted his psychiatrist. Adjusting his medication and increasing his therapy sessions helped Paul avoid a full-blown manic episode and maintain stability.

Chapter 10:

Coping with Depressive Episodes

Identifying Triggers

Understanding and identifying triggers for depressive episodes, such as stress, lack of sleep, or significant life changes, can help in managing them. Keeping a mood diary can help track triggers and symptoms.

Self-Help Techniques

Techniques such as engaging in enjoyable activities, maintaining social connections, and practicing self-compassion can be beneficial. Setting small, achievable goals and celebrating progress can improve motivation and mood.

Professional Support

Therapists and support groups can provide additional support during depressive episodes. Cognitive-behavioural therapy (CBT) can help address negative thought patterns and promote healthier thinking.

Case Study: Anna's Battle with Depression

Anna, a 26-year-old student, struggled with severe depressive episodes that affected her academic performance and social life. Her therapist helped her identify triggers and develop coping strategies. Joining a support group provided Anna with a sense of community and understanding, helping her manage her depressive episodes more effectively.

Chapter 11:

The Role of Support Systems

Family and Friends

A strong support network of family and friends can provide emotional support and practical assistance. Open communication about the condition and its impact can foster understanding and empathy.

Support Groups

Support groups offer a safe space to share experiences and gain insights from others living with bipolar disorder. These groups can provide practical advice, emotional support, and a sense of community.

Community Resources

Community resources, such as mental health organizations and hotlines, can provide additional support. These resources offer information, counselling, and crisis intervention services.

Case Study: Tom's Support Network

Tom, a 50-year-old lawyer, found that his family and friends were crucial in his journey with bipolar disorder. Regular family meetings helped them understand his condition and how to support him effectively. Joining a local support group provided Tom with a platform to share his experiences and learn from others, significantly enhancing his coping mechanisms.

Chapter 12:

Bipolar Disorder in Relationships

Communication

Open and honest communication is key to maintaining healthy relationships. Discussing the impact of bipolar disorder and expressing needs and concerns can foster understanding and support.

Educating Loved Ones

Educating loved ones about bipolar disorder can help them understand and support you better. Providing information about symptoms, treatment, and how they can help can strengthen relationships.

Managing Conflict

Learning effective conflict resolution skills can improve relationship dynamics. Techniques such as active listening, staying calm, and finding mutually agreeable solutions can reduce stress and strengthen bonds.

Case Study: Laura and Mike's Relationship

Laura, a 32-year-old graphic designer, and her partner Mike struggled with the impact of her bipolar disorder on their relationship. Through couples therapy, they learned to communicate more effectively and understand each other's perspectives. Educating Mike about bipolar disorder helped him provide better support, improving their relationship dynamics.

Chapter 13:

Navigating Work and Bipolar Disorder

Workplace Accommodations

Understanding your rights and seeking appropriate workplace accommodations can help you manage bipolar disorder at work. Flexible hours, modified workloads, and regular breaks can reduce stress and improve productivity.

Managing Stress

Implementing stress management techniques can improve work performance and reduce the risk of mood episodes. Techniques such as mindfulness, time management, and setting realistic goals can help manage work-related stress.

Career Planning

Choosing a career that aligns with your strengths and managing stress levels can contribute to long-term success. Finding a supportive work environment and balancing work with self-care is crucial.

Case Study: Kevin's Career Adjustment

Kevin, a 42-year-old software developer, struggled with managing his bipolar disorder in a high-stress work environment. After discussing his condition with his employer, Kevin was able to adjust his workload and schedule to better manage his symptoms. This accommodation, along with stress management techniques, helped Kevin maintain his job and improve his well-being.

Chapter 14:

Long-Term Management and Prognosis

Treatment Adherence

Adhering to treatment plans, including medication and therapy, is crucial for long-term management. Regular follow-ups with healthcare providers ensure that treatment remains effective.

Monitoring Symptoms

Regularly monitoring symptoms and maintaining open communication with healthcare providers can help manage the condition. Keeping a mood diary and tracking symptoms can provide valuable insights.

Preventing Relapse

Strategies to prevent relapse include maintaining a stable routine, avoiding triggers, and seeking support when needed. Early intervention and proactive management can reduce the risk of relapse.

Case Study: Rachel's Long-Term Management

Rachel, a 37-year-old pharmacist, learned the importance of adhering to her treatment plan after experiencing several relapses. Regularly attending therapy sessions, monitoring her symptoms, and maintaining a stable routine helped Rachel achieve long-term stability and improve her quality of life.

Chapter 15:

Personal Stories and Inspiration

Stories of Resilience

Hearing from others who have successfully managed bipolar disorder can provide inspiration and hope. Personal stories highlight the challenges and triumphs of living with bipolar disorder and the strategies that have helped others.

Overcoming Stigma

Addressing and overcoming the stigma associated with bipolar disorder is crucial for improving mental health outcomes. Sharing personal stories and promoting awareness can help reduce stigma and foster a more supportive environment.

Finding Purpose

Living with bipolar disorder can be challenging, but finding purpose and meaning in life can provide motivation and resilience. Engaging in meaningful activities, setting goals, and building supportive relationships can enhance well-being.

Case Study: Michael's Inspirational Journey

Michael, a 55-year-old musician, faced significant challenges due to his bipolar disorder. Through perseverance, support from loved ones, and effective treatment, Michael found stability and continued to pursue his passion for music. His story of resilience and determination serves as an inspiration to others facing similar challenges.

Chapter 16:

Parenting with Bipolar Disorder

Managing Parenting Responsibilities

Balancing parenting responsibilities with managing bipolar disorder can be challenging. Developing a routine, seeking support, and prioritizing self-care can help manage these demands.

Communicating with Children

Open and age-appropriate communication with children about bipolar disorder can help them understand and cope. Providing reassurance and addressing their concerns is crucial.

Seeking Support

Support from family, friends, and professional caregivers can help in managing parenting responsibilities. Joining support groups for parents with bipolar disorder can provide additional resources and emotional support.

Case Study: Emma's Parenting Journey

Emma, a 40-year-old mother of two, found it challenging to balance her parenting responsibilities with managing her bipolar disorder. By developing a routine, seeking support from her family, and joining a support group, Emma learned to manage her responsibilities more effectively and maintain stability.

Chapter 17:

Bipolar Disorder and Creativity

The Link Between Bipolar Disorder and Creativity

There is a well-documented link between bipolar disorder and creativity. Many individuals with bipolar disorder have reported heightened creativity during manic or hypomanic episodes. Understanding this connection can provide insights into the strengths and challenges associated with the disorder.

Harnessing Creativity

Harnessing creativity in a structured way can provide a therapeutic outlet and enhance well-being. Engaging in creative activities, such as writing, painting, or music, can help manage symptoms and improve mood.

Managing Creative Bursts

Managing creative bursts involves balancing the drive to create with the need for stability. Setting realistic goals, maintaining a routine, and seeking feedback from others can help manage creative energy.

Case Study: Michael's Creative Journey

Michael, a 55-year-old musician, found that his creative bursts often coincided with his manic episodes. By learning to channel his creativity into structured activities and seeking feedback from his peers, Michael was able to harness his creative energy while maintaining stability.

Chapter 18:

Personal Stories and Inspiration

Stories of Resilience

Hearing from others who have successfully managed bipolar disorder can provide inspiration and hope. Personal stories highlight the challenges and triumphs of living with bipolar disorder and the strategies that have helped others.

Overcoming Stigma

Addressing and overcoming the stigma associated with bipolar disorder is crucial for improving mental health outcomes. Sharing personal stories and promoting awareness can help reduce stigma and foster a more supportive environment.

Finding Purpose

Living with bipolar disorder can be challenging, but finding purpose and meaning in life can provide motivation and resilience. Engaging in meaningful activities, setting goals, and building supportive relationships can enhance well-being.

Case Study: Michael's Inspirational Journey

Michael, a 55-year-old musician, faced significant challenges due to his bipolar disorder. Through perseverance, support from loved ones, and effective treatment, Michael found stability and continued to pursue his passion for music. His story of resilience

Living with Bipolar Disorder

and determination serves as an inspiration to others facing similar challenges.

This comprehensive guide offers a detailed look into the various aspects of living with bipolar disorder, from diagnosis and treatment to managing daily life and finding hope. By incorporating case studies and practical advice, it aims to provide valuable insights and support to those affected by this condition. Each chapter provides in-depth information, ensuring that readers have the tools and knowledge to navigate the complexities of bipolar disorder and lead fulfilling lives.

Living with Bipolar Disorder

Courtney Collins

Living with Bipolar Disorder

Printed in Great Britain
by Amazon